THE MAKING OF
BLACK PANTHER

KENNY ABDO

Fly!
An Imprint of Abdo Zoom
abdobooks.com

abdobooks.com

Published by Abdo Zoom, a division of ABDO, P.O. Box 398166, Minneapolis, Minnesota 55439. Copyright © 2024 by Abdo Consulting Group, Inc. International copyrights reserved in all countries. No part of this book may be reproduced in any form without written permission from the publisher. Fly!™ is a trademark and logo of Abdo Zoom.

Printed in the United States of America, North Mankato, Minnesota.
052023
092023

THIS BOOK CONTAINS
RECYCLED MATERIALS

Photo Credits: Alamy, Everett Collection. Getty Images, Shutterstock
Production Contributors: Kenny Abdo, Jennie Forsberg, Grace Hansen
Design Contributors: Candice Keimig, Neil Klinepier, Colleen McLaren

Library of Congress Control Number: 2022946923

Publisher's Cataloging-in-Publication Data

Names: Abdo, Kenny, author.
Title: The making of Black Panther / by Kenny Abdo
Description: Minneapolis, Minnesota : Abdo Zoom, 2024 | Series: Blockbusters | Includes online resources and index.
Identifiers: ISBN 9781098281298 (lib. bdg.) | ISBN 9781098281991 (ebook) | ISBN 9781098282349 (Read-to-me ebook)
Subjects: LCSH: Motion pictures--Juvenile literature. | Filmmaking (Motion pictures)--Juvenile literature. | Black Panther (Motion picture : 2018)--Juvenile literature. | Motion pictures--Production and direction—Juvenile literature.
Classification: DDC 791.43--dc23

TABLE OF CONTENTS

BLACK PANTHER

Marvel's *Black Panther* has its claws in movie history as one of the biggest solo superhero **blockbusters** ever!

The 2018 film earned more than $1 billion and became the first superhero movie to be nominated for the Best Picture **Academy Award**!

LIGHTS, CAMERA, ...

Black Panther had been in the works since the 1990s. In 2016, Marvel announced that Ryan Coogler would write and direct the movie. Chadwick Boseman would star.

At nine years old, Coogler went into his local comic shop. He asked for a superhero that "looked like him." Coogler was handed *Black Panther*. The rest is history.

ACTION!

Coogler wanted to explore the theme of identity. "That's something I've always struggled with as a person," he said. "'Who are you?' is a question that comes up a lot in this film."

Chadwick Boseman was the only actor considered for T'Challa. He was already a trained fighter. But Boseman had to learn the Wakanda **dialect**. It was based on the **Xhosa** language.

Production designer Hannah Beachler created a 515-page history of Wakanda covering more than 10,000 years.

Beachler became the first Black person to be nominated and win the Best Production Design **Oscar**.

The fighting in *Black Panther* is based on African martial arts. Ruth E. Carter created over 1,000 costumes for the film. She drew **inspiration** from traditional African tribal clothing.

LEGACY

Black Panther won three **Academy Awards**! *Black Panther: Wakanda Forever* was released in 2022. The film stars Letitia Wright as Shuri. It mourns the death of King T'Challa and pays tribute to Chadwick Boseman.

Boseman sadly passed away in 2020 after battling with **cancer**. His portrayal of T'Challa and the *Black Panther* franchise will continue to inspire generations to come.

GLOSSARY

Academy Awards – one of several awards the Academy of Motion Picture Arts and Sciences gives annually to achievement in the movie industry.

blockbuster – a movie that is incredibly popular and makes a lot of money.

cancer – a disease in which certain cells divide and grow much faster than they normally do.

dialect – a form of a language spoken in a certain area or by certain people.

inspiration – to gain motivation or creativity from another source.

Oscar – another name for an Academy Award.

production designer – the head of the art department. Responsible for bringing the director's ideas to life and the overall visual appearance and artistic style of a movie.

Xhosa – a language spoken primarily in South Africa and Zimbabwe.

ONLINE RESOURCES

Booklinks
NONFICTION NETWORK
FREE! ONLINE NONFICTION RESOURCES

To learn more about the making of *Black Panther*, please visit abdobooklinks.com or scan this QR code. These links are routinely monitored and updated to provide the most current information available.

INDEX